EDWARD CULLINAN
ARCHITECTS

RIBA Publications Limited

Preface

The buildings shown in this book are
generally unannotated. But they have been
laid out to give as clear a story as possible,
through drawings and pictures. They are
also arranged under seven chapter headings;
at each chapter page there is a written
description of the buildings in that chapter.

Photographs
References are to page numbers

Geremy Butler 87
Graham Challifour 39, 41 (top left)
Martin Charles 66, 67, 69, 78, 83, 85. 90, 91
Stuart Haden 60, 61
Brian Housden 11
John Sturrock 37, 71
Bill Toomey 75, 77
Mark Wickham 18, 23, 25, 53, 55, 56 (top left, bottom
right), 57

Introduction

The work of Edward Cullinan Architects, noticed in high and other places, hardly needs an Introduction at all – particularly by one who is unaccustomed to many of the ways of the real world (though not its vagaries). And to be attempting an Introduction from beyond the Atlantic invites speculations that may be too academic as I have to rely on memory and other people's pictures. Nevertheless, it is with a swell of pride, having been asked to do it, that I undertake the task!

Being at such a distance (I am in Toronto), I am reminded of that, perhaps apocryphal, observation made by a visitor from a very different culture on first being in New York City. That visitor was impressed, at the expense of everything else, by the brass knobs which capped so many newel-posts – being, some time ago, a standard commercial stair detail. As a regular visitor to Cullinan Country (I have to go through Marlborough to reach it), I have noted the water butts! Like the visitor to New York, I am sure I should have noticed other, perhaps more significant, things. But, to be truthful, the Cullinan butts *are* very noticeable! Nevertheless, they are just one of the many discrete things that lend their presence to the Cullinan scene. They are there in the early projects – the lighthouse and the solid elements of the early houses – as they are in the most recent – the toilet drums of the Uplands Conference Centre or the caretaker's house in the Streatham project.

These vessels of reserve, the drums and the butts, remind me of the Dogon granaries, which, since Aldo van Eyck brought them back, are familiar images for architects. To be reminded of the granaries is useful in two ways. Firstly, and more importantly, they stand as a testament of a culture. They manifest the ethos of Dogon culture just as the water butts manifest the Cullinan ethos – for example, they become agents to our understanding of the seasons and good husbandry. Secondly, the granaries, like Cullinan buildings, are carefully placed upon the ground, being of it, while their roofs, often at a somewhat coquettish angle, speak more of the sky.

The work in this catalogue represents such an ethos: there is an order (dare I say 'architecture'?) in which everything is all-of-a-piece with everything else. Just like farms where any one building may stand as an agent for the whole. This sensibility in the work of Edward Cullinan Architects is, for me, its most rewarding aspect – it speaks of intelligence! The Cullinan ethos holds everything in place – the co-operative office, the declared authorship of each project and, of course, the consistency of the projects themselves. Seeing a Cullinan building, I think 'Of course!' and chide myself for not having seen things that way and that '*Of course!*' is a curse for Romantic Pragmatists, just as intelligence is. I believe the recent dubbing, by parties in high and other places, does not go to the heart of the Cullinan matter.

Unfortunately, there is a risk in having such an order – an ethos – no matter how intelligent it may be. Too often, in moments of relaxation, the grass on other cultures will seem greener! I feel there has been a slight ache for another culture when I notice some of the water butts have been overlayed with other tasks. In a few projects, for example, they are made to serve as Home Guards or symbolic gate-posts. But to say this is to recognise the effort, throughout a considerable body of work, that has gone into the definition and refinement of the order! It is an effort of clarification of the context of each problem (buildings, I believe, are mostly determined by their authors' perception of the problems they are given), just as it is an effort of three-dimensional construction.

As a visitor, I have been privileged to be, from time to time, within the Cullinan order. In their house near Leek, it is possible to live in a peer-relation, not only with the Cullinans, but with the water butts, the shower, the stove, the roof beams – with *all* the apparatus of their scene. Such a scene is a whole landscape and being in it, it is possible to experience the extraordinary vitality and enthusiastic comprehensiveness that informs, and is the hall-mark of, Cullinan-inspired order. And in the same landscape it is possible to see the Cullinans' other, similar, endeavour – they coax things to grow in a climate somewhat less than benign (and one that has largely defeated the ambitions of local cultivators and agriculturalists).

It is no secret that Ted Cullinan greatly admires that other farmer-figure, Berthold Lubetkin. Just as I regret that Lubetkin retired early from architecture, so I am glad that Edward Cullinan Architects are steadfast in these rakish times.

Peter Prangnell
Toronto, August 1984

Contents

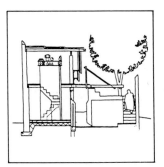
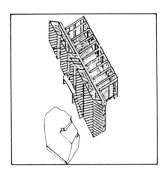
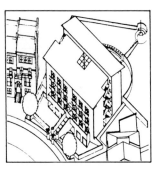
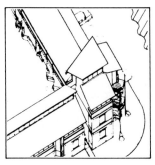
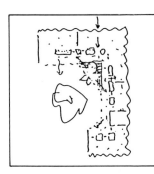
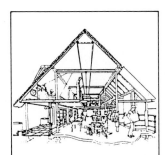

Contents

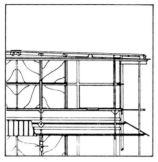
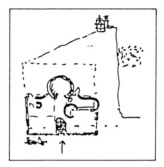

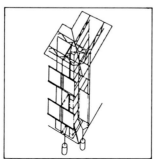

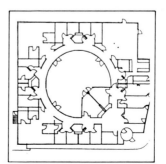

1: Building them yourself

The three houses shown in this chapter were mostly built by me; they are an early part of a habit of building things that has taken hold over the years, and which I share now with many of my workmates.

Detail of Berlarge's Amsterdam Stock Exchange.

I built the house in Hampshire with Max Moodie and a wonderfully adaptable, proud, possessive, 75-year-old gardener named Horace Knight, whose portrait you will see on page 9 in conjunction with a portrait of our combined work: the house in California I built with a young student and my friends, Mariah and Stephen Marvin, for them; and the London house was built with my family and many friends during two years of weekends for us.

I built the buildings more or less myself because I enjoy the sensual process of making things that you can climb about on and later get into; because I am inquisitive about the aesthetics of inventive building construction or the nature of surfaces and connections in the making of spaces (Figure left); and out of an early lust to get things built which otherwise would not have happened.

The process was and is supported by liking the idea of a libertarian world in which people do many different things, by being in California in the fifties at the birth of the hippy era and by the continuous development of products, materials and tools that make it easier to do, year by year, for the thirty years I've done it.

Doing it yourself is also instructive, practically and in arousing empathy with builders, and in that it must constitute the opposite process to the totally understandable advice that I believe Alberti gave; that the architect should never visit the site of his building while under construction, lest sympathy with the problems experienced by the builder should lead him to modify the purity of the design. In this Alberti, humanist though he was,

stressed the cerebral part of the art of building; my early experience stressed the sensual or tactile.

Of course the main thing that limits amateur building is the considerable incapacities of the amateur. This tends to lead to a mode of construction and expression that uses a severely limited range of available materials, puts a stress on 'placed together' joints and junctions, has materials mastering and oversailing one another and avoids the partial sophistication of 'flushness' and hidden detailing.

The next pages are intended to show the use of this direct building method to produce three small houses. The first, in Hampshire, formalises a crease in the landscape between a steep wooded bank and a brookside meadow; it faces South and collects sun; it is long and thin and it redefines the spaces in a small house to try to make a 'There there'. The second, in California, is beside a rock that rolled there off the coastal range towards the Pacific; it is a long redwood gallery with fixed glass and opening walls that contains a bed, a sitting place round a fire, and a dining table, served by a row of little 'green rooms' containing dressing rooms, cloakrooms, entrance, study and kitchen. The third, in London, is built against a party wall along the North side of the site and its 'indoors' and its 'outdoors' are made of the same bits occupying the whole space within the solid frame created by North and South party walls and the ground; it has a private, closed plan downstairs and a long gallery above and the levels are connected three ways, by formal front steps, by internal stair and by a long ramp. It collects sun.

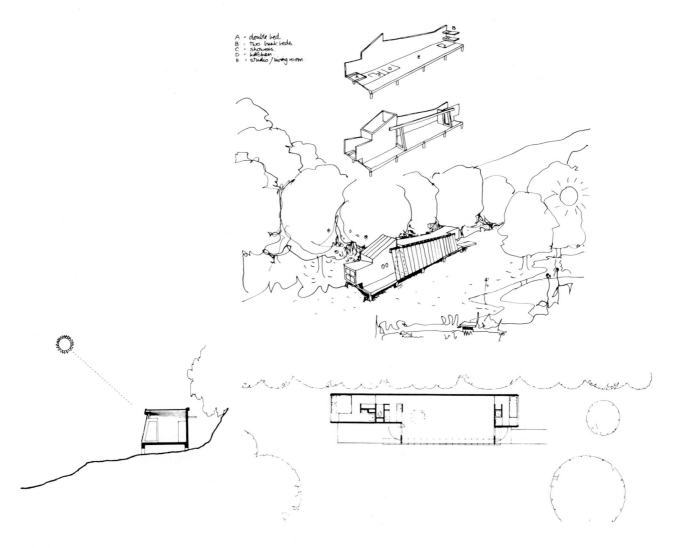

A = double bed.
B = two bunk beds.
C = showers.
D = kitchen.
E = studio / living room.

1959　　　　**HOUSE IN HAMPSHIRE**　　　　**Edward Cullinan**

Horace Knight

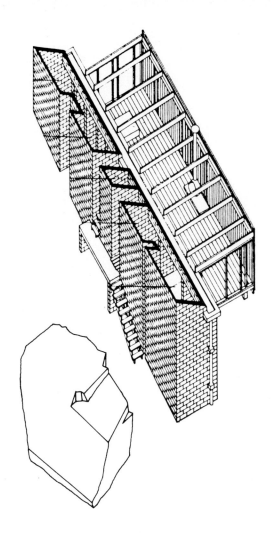

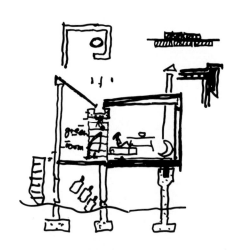

1959

HOUSE IN CALIFORNIA   **Edward Cullinan**

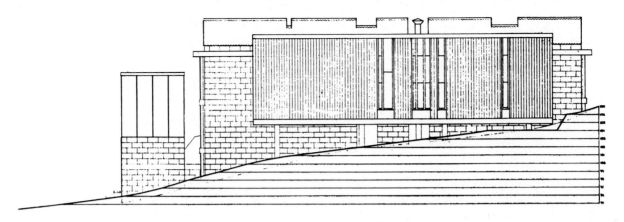

South elevation

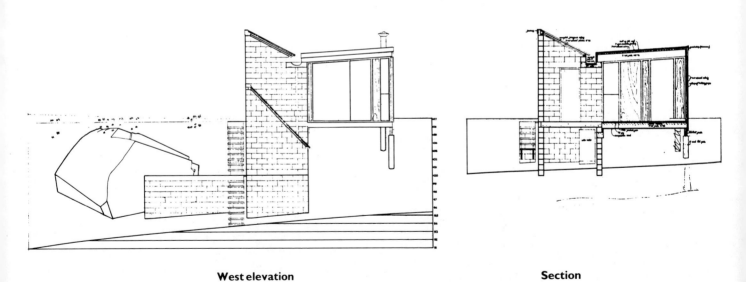

West elevation

Section

THE WORKING DRAWINGS

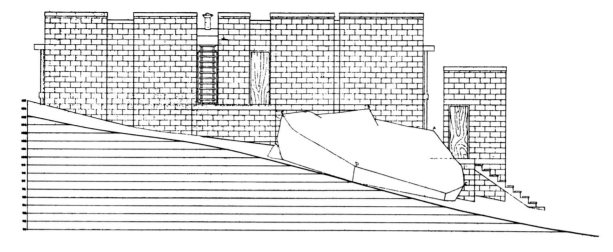

North elevation

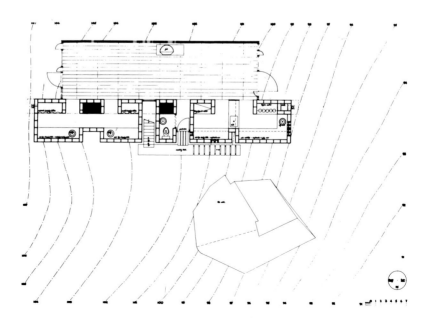

Plan

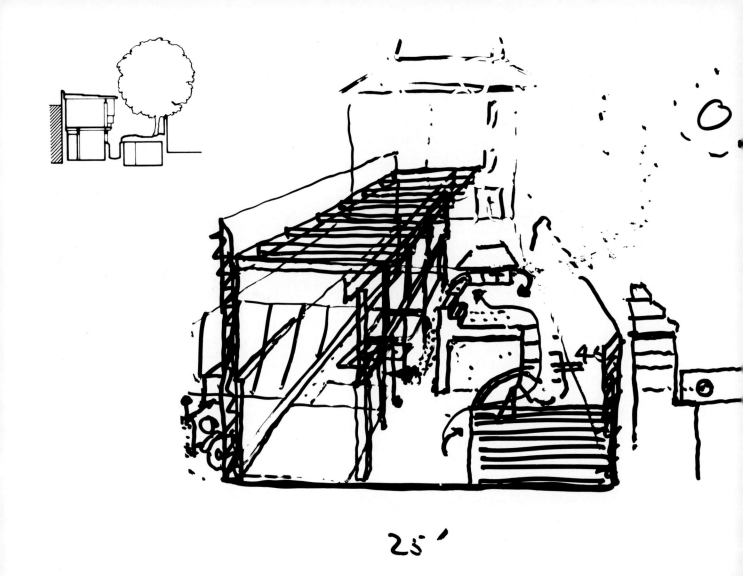

25'

1963

HOUSE IN LONDON **Edward Cullinan**

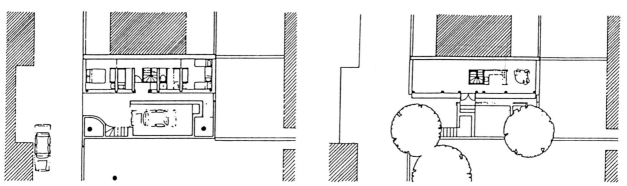

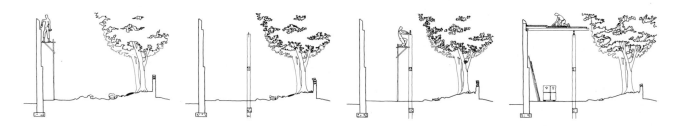

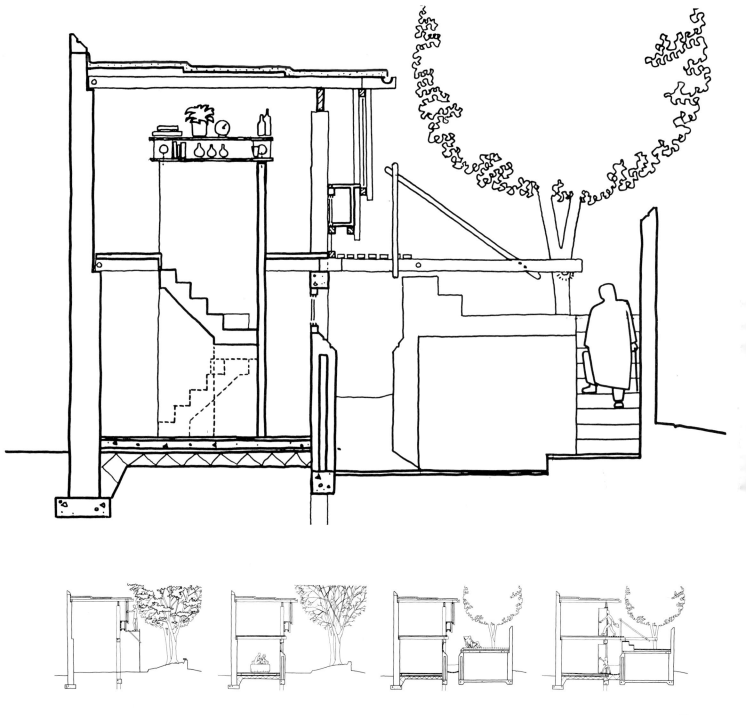

19

2: More and more houses

Important among the issues raised in this chapter are three.

How might the additive, overlapping aesthetic of a 'do it yourself' architecture be more generally applied?

What happens when single houses become a community of houses?

How far can you compensate for being more removed from both building the houses and the people they are built for?

I recently heard Ivan Illich say 'spiders make webs to catch food; cars are parked; only people dwell. In England today very few people dwell; most are parked.' This last point bites deep.

The house on the South Downs (page 22) is a development of the earlier three; in it the main rooms embrace a terrace within the angle of their L and are in turn embraced by lower, solider service rooms that emerge, grass topped from the Downs.

The next two houses, Kawecki (page 24) and Garrett (page 26) are both in the city and are composed into their surroundings. One replaces the bombed off half of an early 19th century villa in North London and it is designed to complete that villa and terminate the row of similar ones: the other makes an end of a long line of early twentieth century semi-detached houses in South London.

On the next two pages (28 and 29) is the story of the development of most of the single houses that I designed and built in the fifties and sixties.

Highgrove (page 30) which is locally known as 'the blue roofs' is in a salubrious North West London suburb and is the first of a series of schemes for local authorities and housing associations. The quadripartite houses are a development of the wide fronted gallery planned earlier houses, with garages, bathrooms, cupboards, stairs and landings in the low back of the section and the main room spaces side by side along the garden frontage. The main room spaces (cooking, eating, sitting) can be used open plan or divided as the occupant chooses and they open onto and 'possess' the garden, forming one of its boundaries. The other garden boundaries are hedged in and these hedges, with the grid of paths and roads and trees make of the site a formal landscape with uneven edges. Highgrove is a radical break with the traditional local authority narrow-fronted house.

Bradwell Common 2 (page 36) in the new city of Milton Keynes and Leighton Crescent (page 38) in London develop different aspects of the Highgrove scheme.

At Bradwell Common, the wide-fronted houses, arranged along a road pattern already established by the city, are designed in seventeen different types and sizes to suit various numbers of people and to celebrate the situations that occur on the site: boulevard, avenue, mews, inward corner, outward corner, hill, opening or portal, end and so on.

At Leighton Crescent, four gallery planned houses and twelve apartments (with movable partitions) form a quadripartite building that both terminates and prolongs the axis of a Victorian crescent. The building itself replaces the missing large-scale centrepiece to the Crescent.

At Westmoreland Road (page 44) in South London thirty-six apartments and duplexes have front doors to a roadside forecourt and an agglomeration of balconies and wide openings to a large shared garden on the South side.

At Nelson Lodge in Basingstoke, a hostel for 100 people, the high building that contains dining rooms and common rooms, forms one side of and shelters the cloistered courtyard of rooms from the high highway behind it.

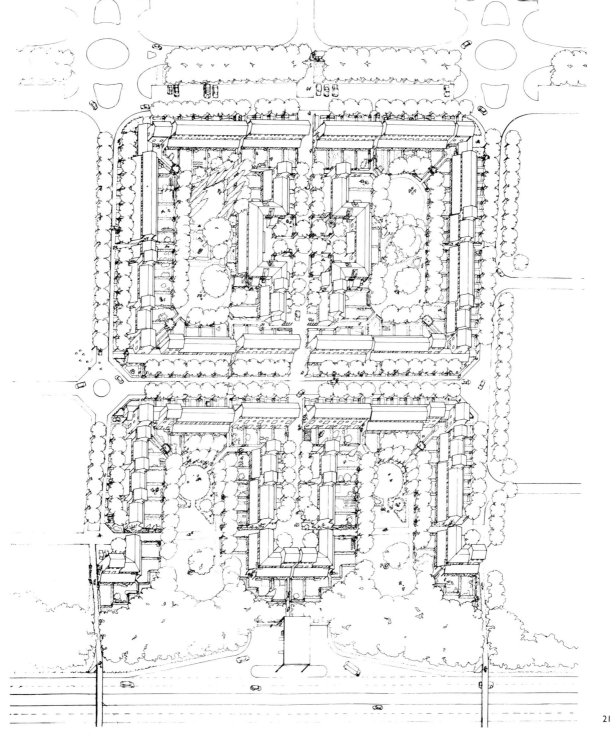

21

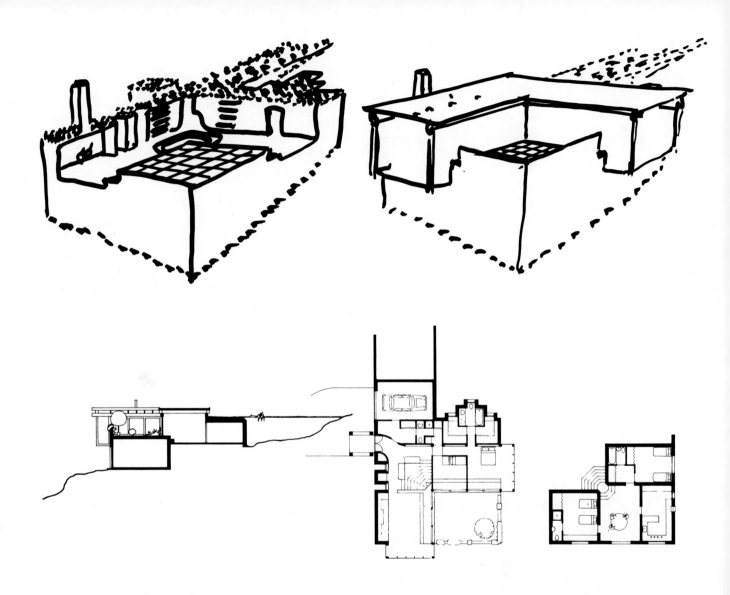

1966

HOUSE ON THE SOUTH DOWNS Edward Cullinan
Alice Milo

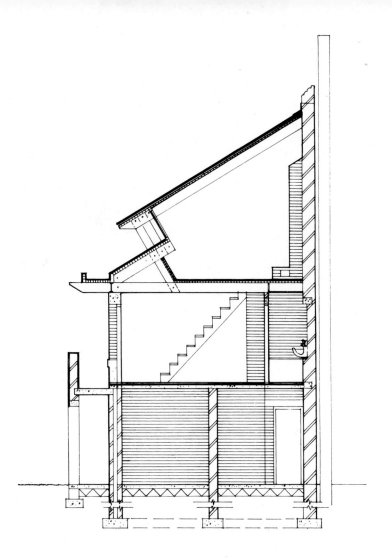

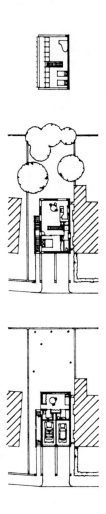

1964

KAWECKI HOUSE, LONDON   **Edward Cullinan**

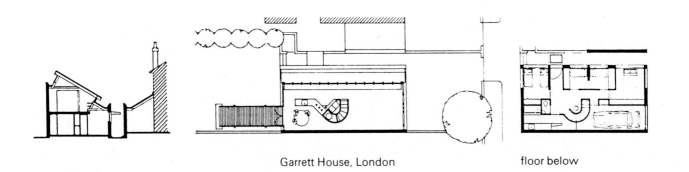

Garrett House, London   floor below

1966   **GARRETT HOUSE, LONDON**   **Edward Cullinan**
                                                     Ian Pickering

Eight houses
1960-70

In 1959/60 we built two houses, one in England and one in California. They were both for people without children and with the resulting simplification we used them to try new arrangements for life within and around them. In the English one, (**1**) we placed two tiny sleeping cabins with their own showers and kit storage at either end to leave the largest possible unnamed living space between them, and we built all those parts against a long north wall to face south. The south side is glass, with screens to hang over it on hot days, to use the English climate as well as we could. The Californian one (**2**) takes further the same big space/small spaces division and provides a long gallery to live in, to eat in and to sleep in, served by accurately planned service 'green rooms' containing cooking, washing and storage of every kind, the essential services for living.

The next three houses we did (**3, 4, 5**) were on small city sites in London and were for families containing numbers of people of all ages. While holding to the long line south facing plans that we think are suitable for the English climate and to developments of the big space/small spaces divisions that we had tried before, we aimed to make plans that would accommodate the mixed joys of family life in a smallish area, cheaply.

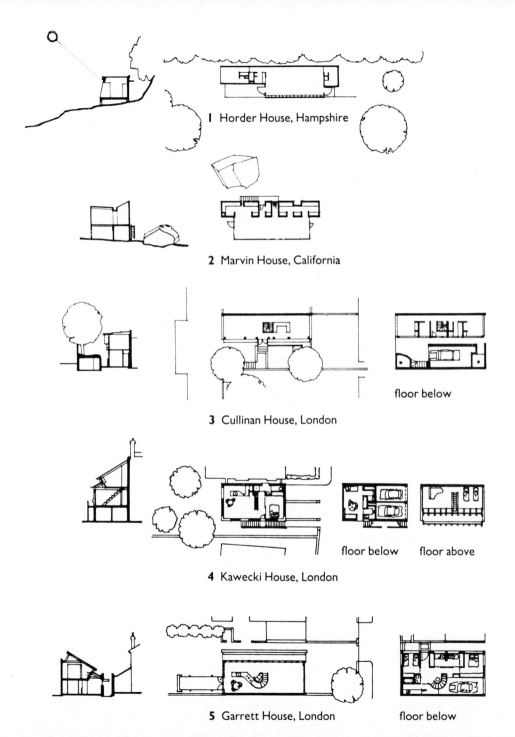

1 Horder House, Hampshire

2 Marvin House, California

3 Cullinan House, London

floor below

4 Kawecki House, London

floor below   floor above

5 Garrett House, London

floor below

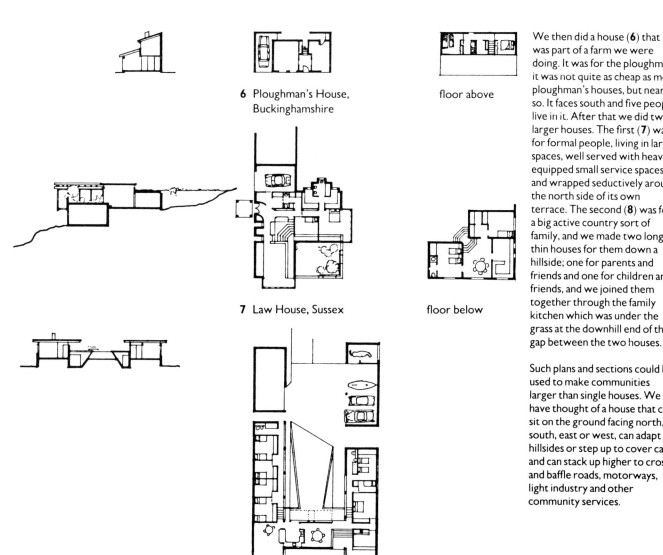

6 Ploughman's House,
Buckinghamshire

floor above

7 Law House, Sussex

floor below

8 Knox House, Suffolk

We then did a house (**6**) that was part of a farm we were doing. It was for the ploughman; it was not quite as cheap as most ploughman's houses, but nearly so. It faces south and five people live in it. After that we did two larger houses. The first (**7**) was for formal people, living in large spaces, well served with heavily equipped small service spaces and wrapped seductively around the north side of its own terrace. The second (**8**) was for a big active country sort of family, and we made two long thin houses for them down a hillside; one for parents and friends and one for children and friends, and we joined them together through the family kitchen which was under the grass at the downhill end of the gap between the two houses.

Such plans and sections could be used to make communities larger than single houses. We have thought of a house that can sit on the ground facing north, south, east or west, can adapt to hillsides or step up to cover cars and can stack up higher to cross and baffle roads, motorways, light industry and other community services.

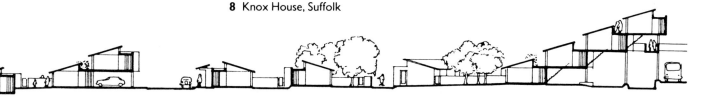

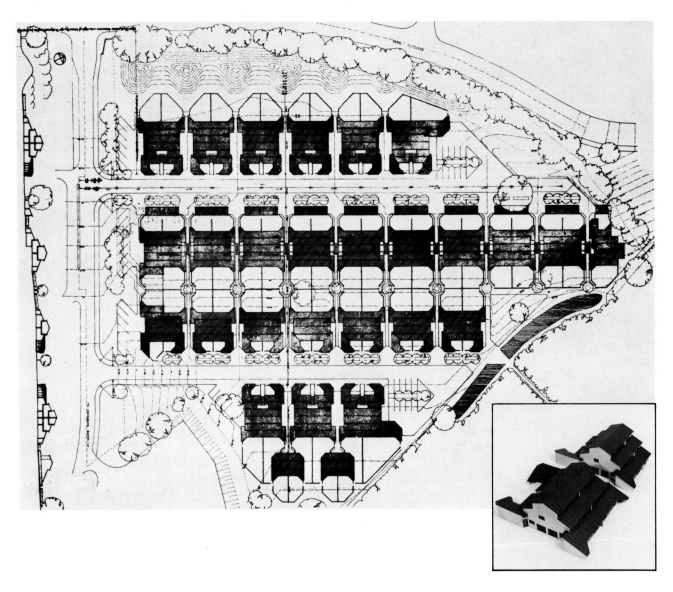

1971

HIGHGROVE (Scheme 3)

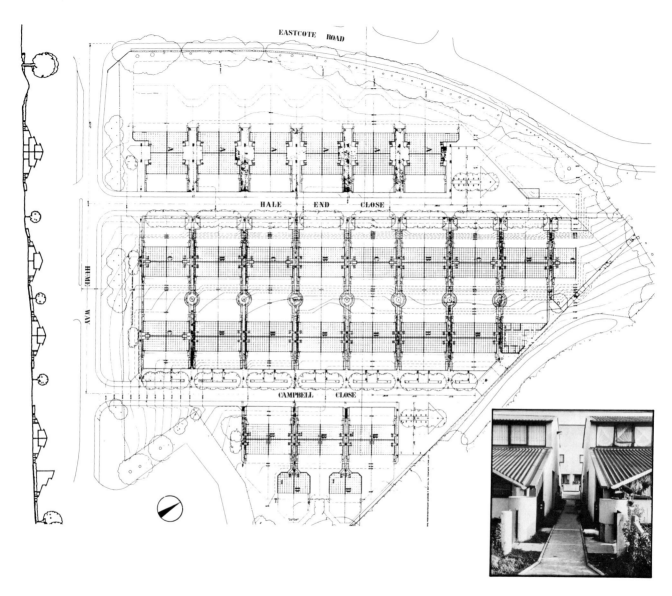

1972

HIGHGROVE (Scheme 4)
AS BUILT

Edward Cullinan
Michael Chassay
Mark Beedle
Brendan Woods
Anthony Peake

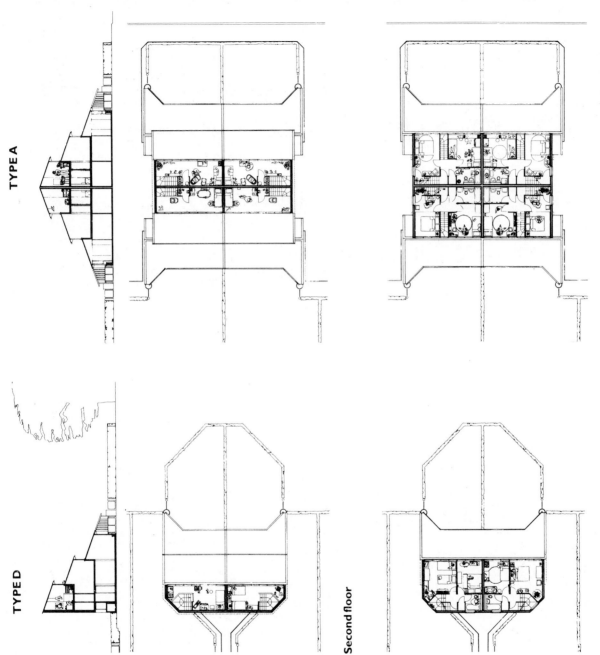

TYPE A

TYPE D

Second floor

First floor

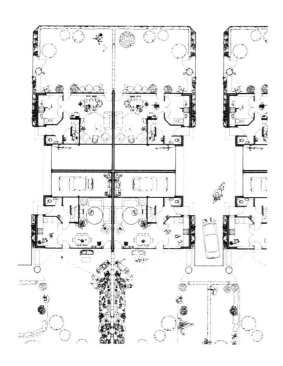

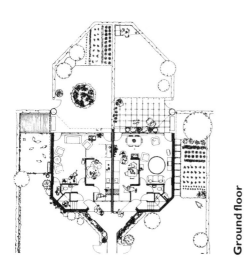

Ground floor

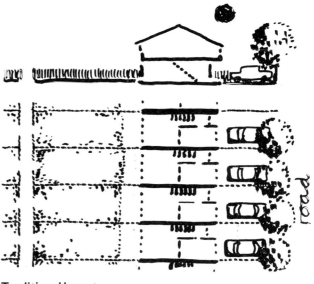

Traditional layout

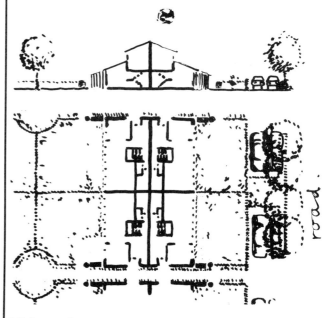

Highgrove layout

33

A house

**Houses that go up a floor
to come down hills**

**Houses, flats and shops
to make corners**

**Houses make valleys
and roads**

Houses make closes

**Houses to face the
upper boulevarde**

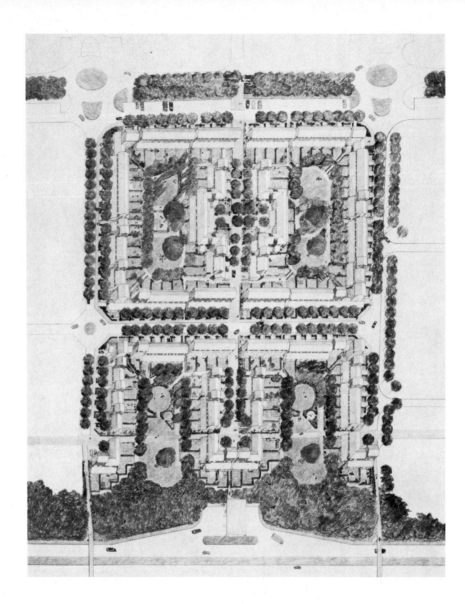

1979

BRADWELL COMMON

**Edward Cullinan
Anthony Peake
Giles Oliver
Michael Chassay
Sunand Prasad**

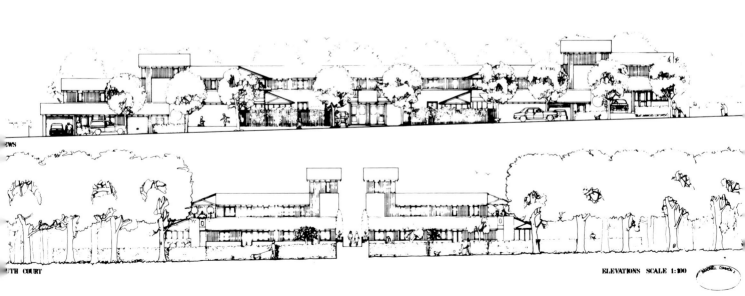

EWS

UTH COURT

ELEVATIONS SCALE 1:100

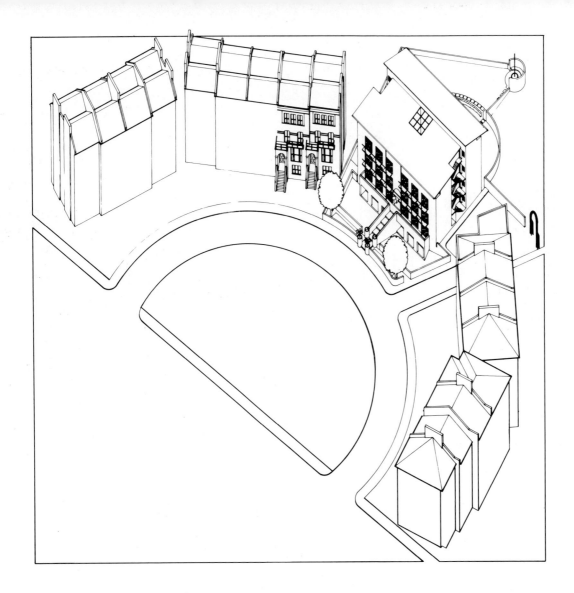

1977

LEIGHTON CRESCENT

Edward Cullinan
Philip Tabor
Michael Chassay
Mark Beedle

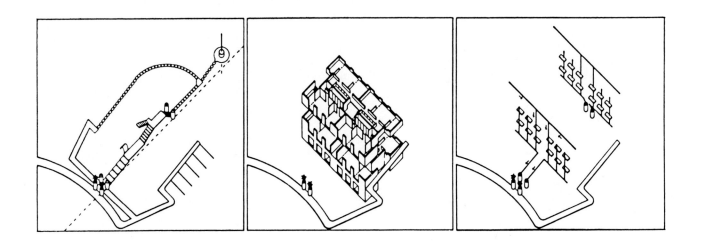

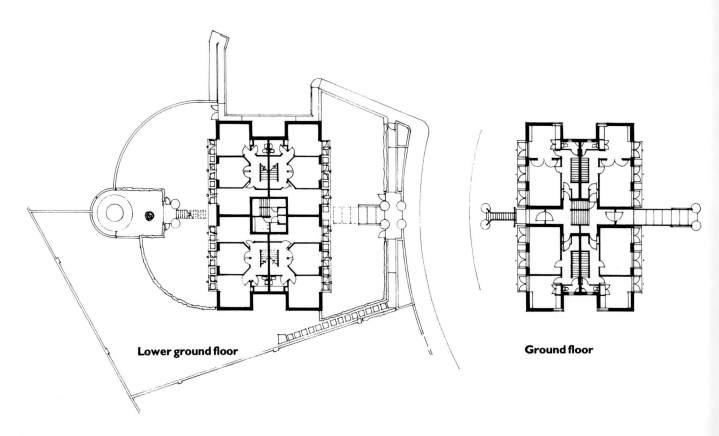

Lower ground floor

Ground floor

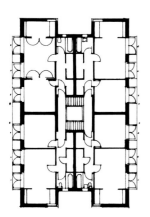
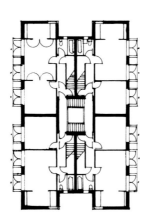
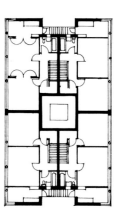

1st floor   **2nd floor**   **3rd floor**

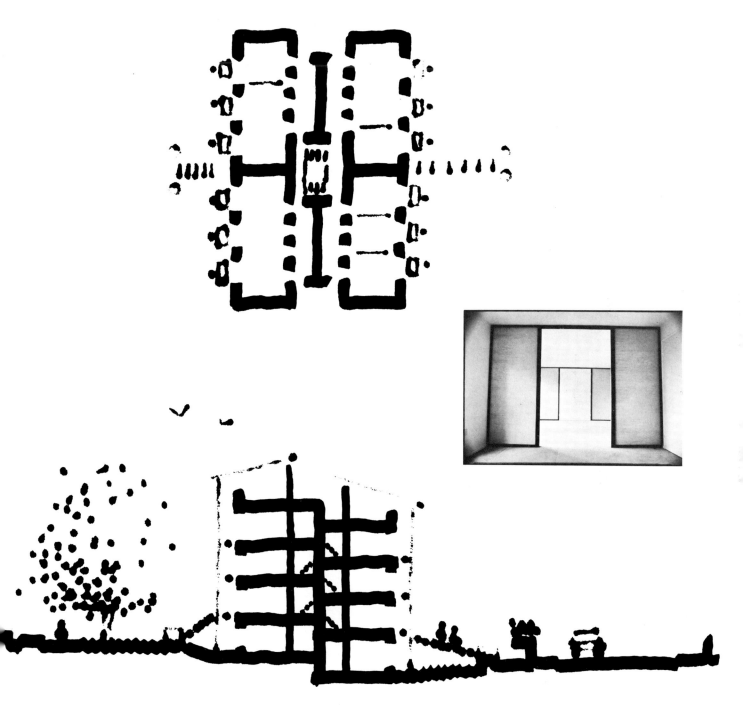

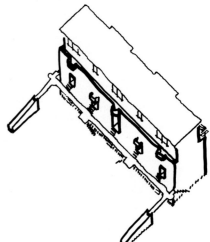

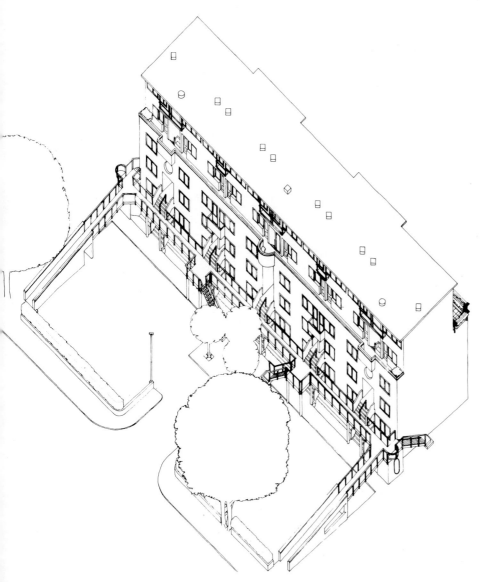

1974-9

WESTMORELAND ROAD

Edward Cullinan
Brendan Woods
Sunand Prasad

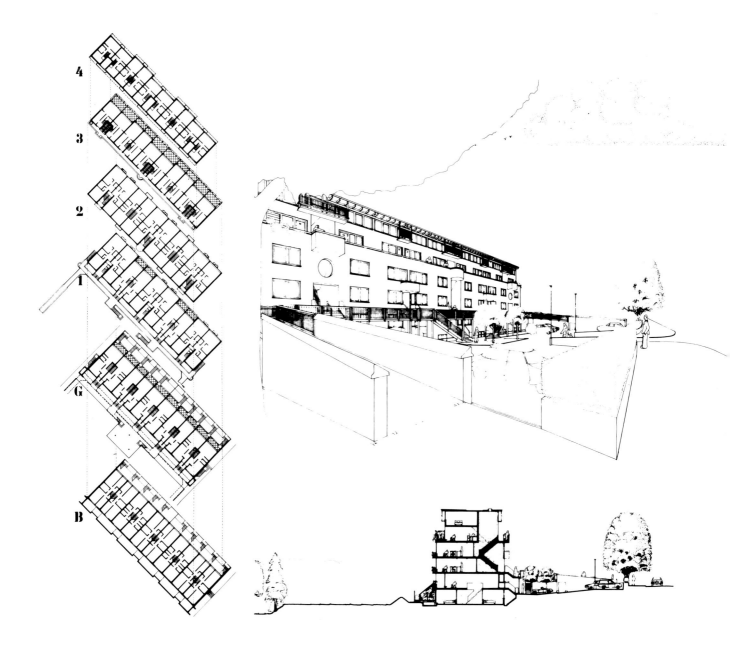

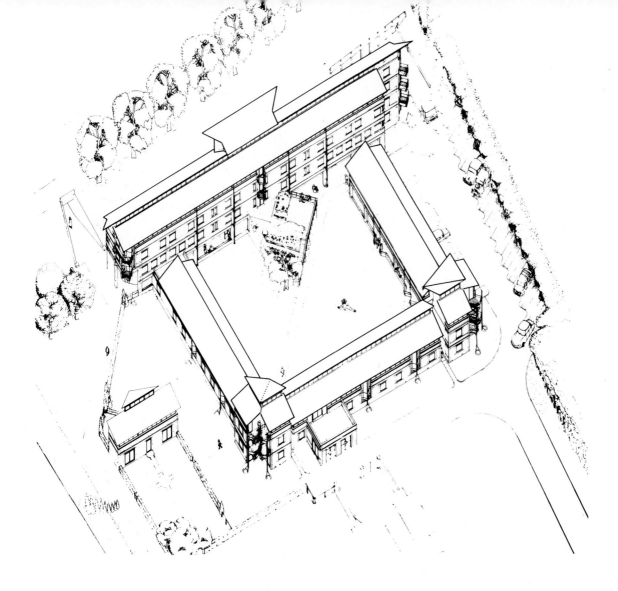

1983

NELSON LODGE

Edward Cullinan
Sunand Prasad
Gregory Penoyre
Frances Holliss

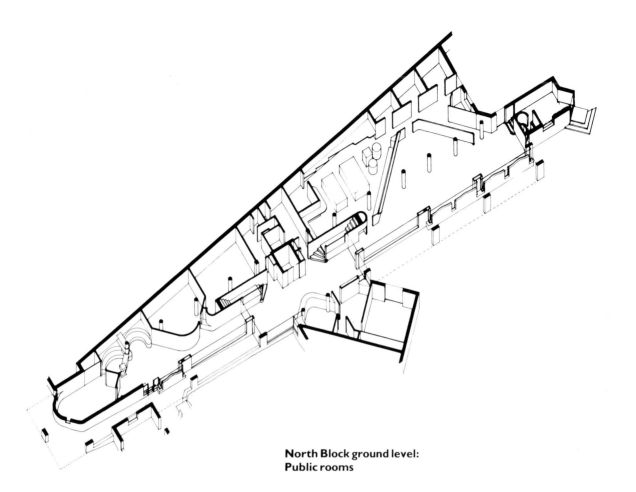

**North Block ground level:
Public rooms**

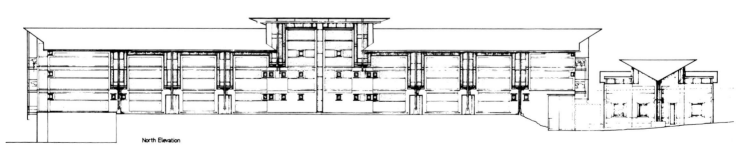

North Elevation

Street elevation

3: Workshops

In the late sixties and early seventies, we made a series of buildings in Britain for Olivetti. Most were conversions, but four were new branches – in Dundee, Derby, Belfast and Carlisle.

Pages 52 to 57 describe those buildings, concentrating on the Dundee building; the picture on the opposite page is an interior view of the Carlisle building after its recent conversion into quite a good Chinese restaurant. I hope that the following description of the buildings will make it clear why and how they might be used as a restaurant or for other purposes as well as for the combination of showroom, sales rooms, offices, workshops and storage that Olivetti originally asked for.

All four buildings are on pieces of leftover ground or on industrial estates on the outskirts of their cities, and they are designed to make places or oases on and within those nondescript locations. They are built from a standard set of components in different shapes to suit each site.

The lower storey, of concrete masonry construction, is a kind of above-ground basement or foundation for the main floor above; it contains front and back entrances and cloakrooms, electrical and mechanical services rooms, waste disposal, deliveries and the storage of machines: outside these spaces, nosed in under the edge of the building, are parked the cars of the workers, buyers and sellers. The lower storey is traditionally built so as to be able to flex to deal with the peculiar conditions of each site; width and length, position of road access, pedestrian access, planning requirements and so on. But in each case, the lower storey establishes the basic form of the building, a U which presents a whole side to the main road and has tails that go up the sides of the site for as far as the present accommodation requires.

Entering through the lower storey, you rise into the mezzanine in an angle of the 'U'; the mezzanine is both a foyer and the social centre of the building. The main floor, a U with two temporary ends awaiting future expansion, contains circulation as an extension of the mezzanine along its inside edge, glazed and public to its private courtyard. Outside the circulation strip is a further 2m wide strip of entrances and flexible storage space, and beyond that, along the long outside of the building, lie the offices, showrooms and workshops,

dividable at 4m intervals, open plan or closed but usually a mixture of both, as chosen by the individual branch managers.

This main floor is constructed from a repeated kit of steel and plywood parts, devised by us and built dry onto the platform prepared for it on top of the lower, service storey.

Also on this page is a side elevation of the workshop that we made for the MacIntyre Schools for mentally handicapped children and young adults in Bedfordshire; the larger building is the workshop that forms one side of a courtyard, the smaller one is a house for the same children (with adults upstairs) that makes a corner for the court. The workshop (pages 58 to 61) is at right angles to an old building that forms the first side of the court; its tiled pitched roof is a response to the manner in which that building occupies space; but the workshop's interior is an orthogonal steel frame that makes a heavy machine shop on the ground with galleries for crafts above. The simple section of the general space workshop is crossed to make the particular space of the house which thereby makes the first corner of the courtyard.

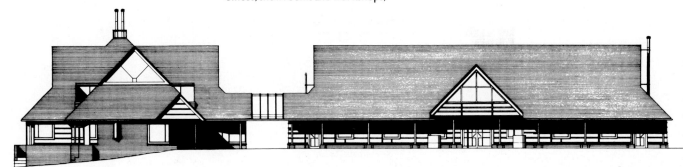

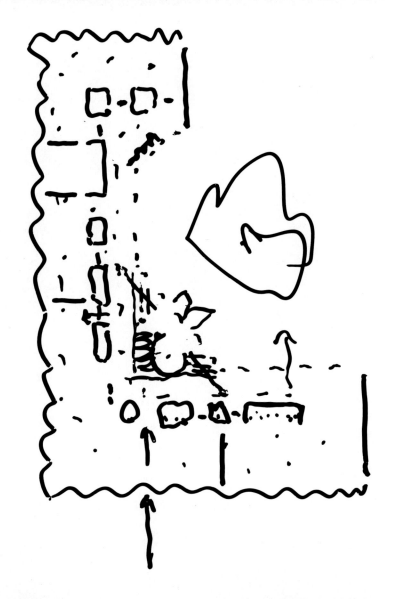

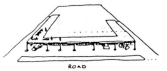

ROAD

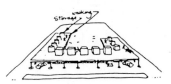

Storage

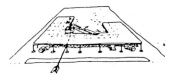

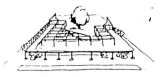

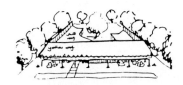

1971

OLIVETTI'S NEW BRANCHES

Edward Cullinan
Julyan Wickham
Michael Chassay
Giles Oliver
Julian Bicknell

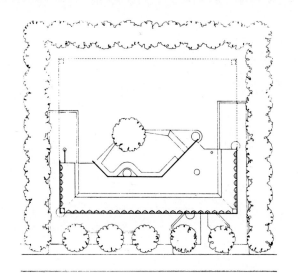

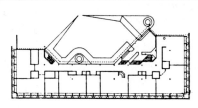

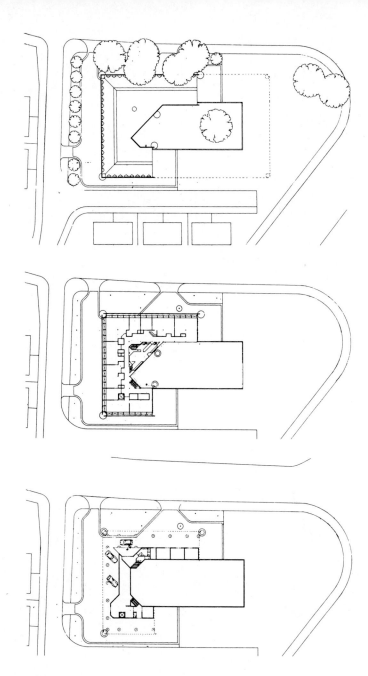

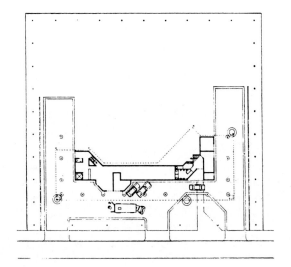

Derby

Belfast

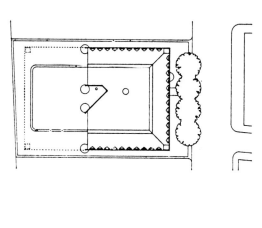

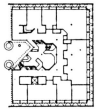

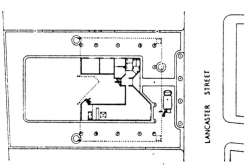

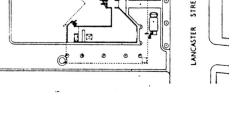

LANCASTER STREET

Carlisle

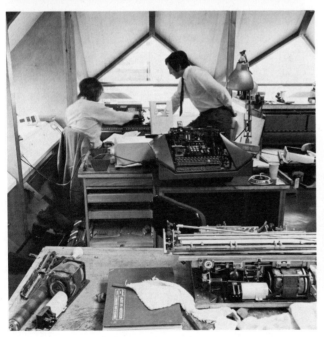

1980-4

WESTONING MANOR

Edward Cullinan
Michael Chassay
Robin Nicholson
Gregory Penoyre

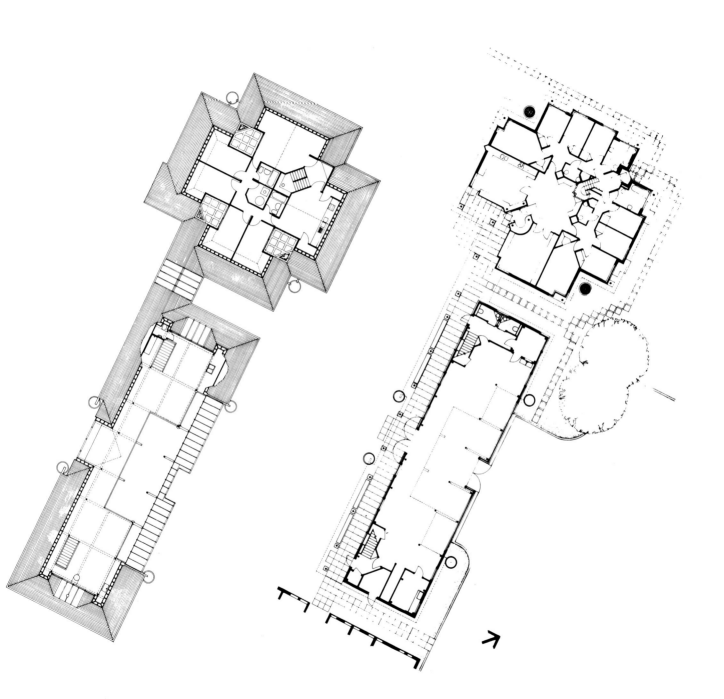

4: Designing in public

The design and rebuilding of Barnes Parish Church in South London (pages 64 to 69) has taken since June 1978, when the old church was burned down, until this week (July 1984) when the last of the furniture was installed.

The church that burned down was a small mediaeval tower nave and chancel that had become the South aisle of a much larger early twentieth century late Gothic Revival nave and North aisle. The heat of the fire was engulfed by the heat of the controversy over how to rebuild it in the local community, and far beyond it. For Barnes, unusually among inner London Victorian suburbs, possessed an old church in an historic churchyard, in Church Road, opposite a village green with duck ponds in it: a series of elements of enormous importance to the place and a buttress to the pleasant fiction that a suburb is a village. There were many noisy, passionate public meetings, attended by hundreds at a time, and we presented many schemes and variations to those meetings, to the ten different bodies who had a say in the matter of this emotive building and to two successive Consistory Courts of the Church of England presided over by the Bishop and his Chancellor to deal with challenges to our application for a faculty to build. And naturally enough, the fundamental division was between those who wanted to rebuild the church more or less as it was including the twentieth century parts and those who wanted to restore the mediaeval church and treat the rest in a more radical way.

If one is to understand the course of history to be inevitably in the direction of a greater public share in the design of their buildings and if we are to embrace this need, it seems to me that three things should be remembered.
(1) One should go to the first meeting with drawings or a model of a scheme to which one has committed the whole of one's understanding so far.
(2) One should describe it very carefully and then listen very carefully for among much heated comment there are gems that are sometimes a valuable source of inspiration.
(3) Having listened and learned, one should then produce a variation or another scheme as a result of the working of public feeling on one's own capacity; to make another proposal that is from within, and not a collection of suggested features. Suggested features will always be numerous but they are only fragments, and cannot of themselves compose a good building. Good buildings are in the future; they must be more than a repetition of the present.

Now Barnes Church is there: a restored mediaeval church stands in its own churchyard; out of it, grows the new nave and crossing, transepts and lantern, geometrically consistent but without pastiche. Nobody can remember what all the fuss was about.

Opposite this page is a detailed photograph of a column capital at the indoor/outdoor adventure playground for handicapped and other children on a large housing estate in Central London. The capital is a steel caryatid or telemon and each column has a different boy on top of it: they are painted different colours and are used to hang things off. Pages 70 and 71 illustrate the building that makes its own North boundary and shelters its own playful landscape.

On pages 72 and 73 is our community care centre, a small cottage hospital in Lambeth, devised during two years of active discussion and steadily developing proposals with local doctors, nurses, community workers, health service officials and future users. Wards are above day patients' rooms, a conservatory with ramps and waterfalls in it connects the levels and so does the garden that grows from the building. It is now under construction.

I MID 12TH C.

II EARLY 13TH C.

III LATE 15TH C.

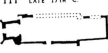

IV LATE 18TH C.

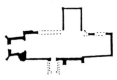

V LATE 18TH C.

VI MID 19TH C.

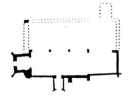

VII EARLY 20TH C.

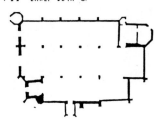

VIII LATE 20TH C.

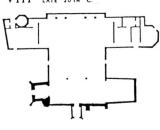

0   20 M

1978-84

BARNES CHURCH

Edward Cullinan
Mark Beedle
Alan Short

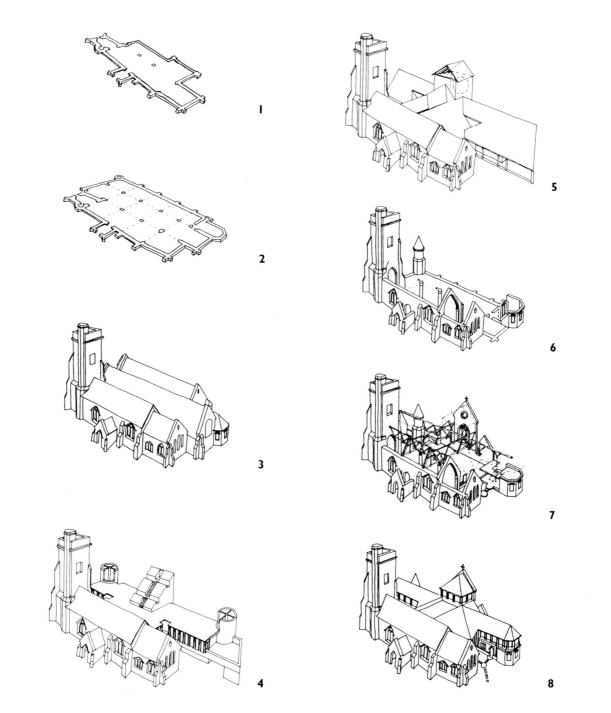

1

2

3

4

5

6

7

8

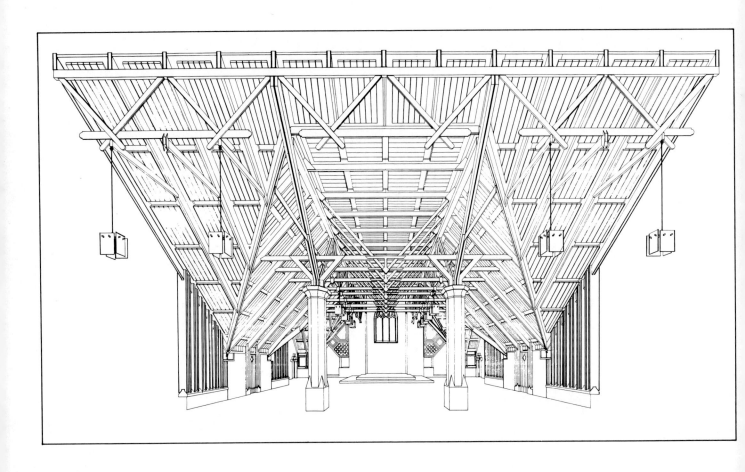

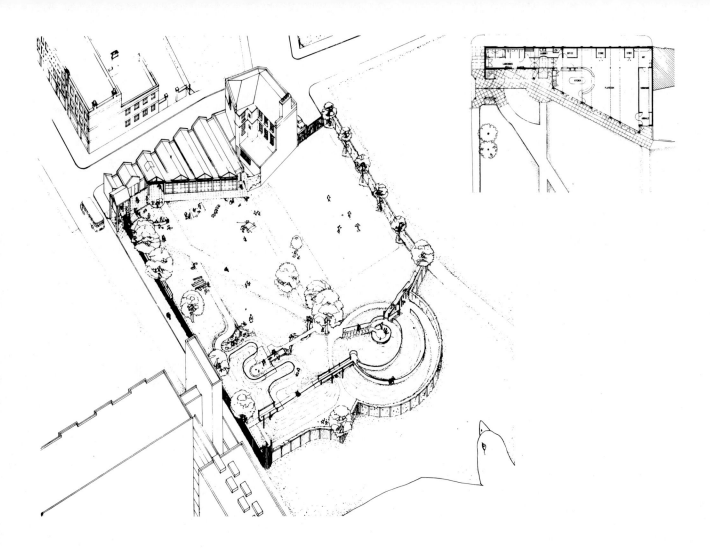

1982

CHARLIE CHAPLIN ADVENTURE PLAYGROUND

**Edward Cullinan
Sunand Prasad
Mungo Smith**

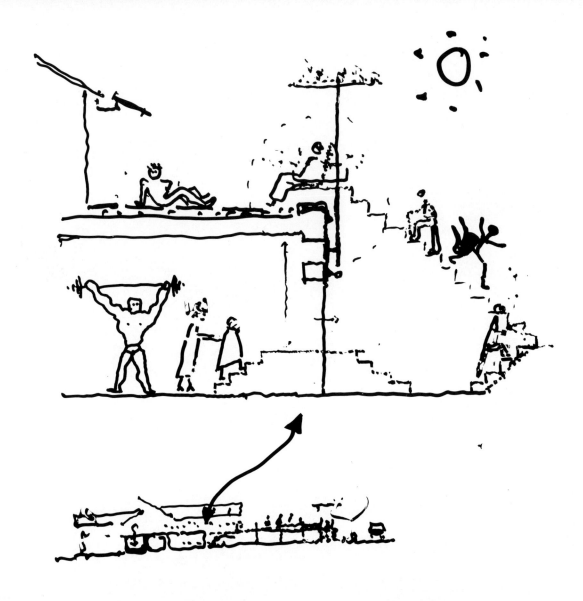

1983

LAMBETH HOSPITAL

Edward Cullinan
Robin Nicholson
Mungo Smith

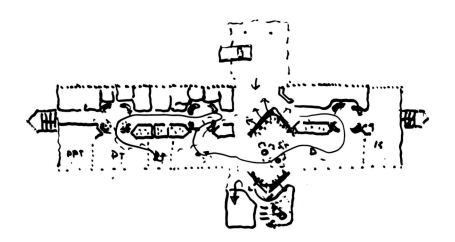

5: Working with old buildings

This survey of our work with old buildings starts at the Minster Lovell Conference Centre; it is shown in interior detail on the opposite page and as a scheme overleaf, on pages 76 and 77.

In the sixties, especially at schools of architecture, there was much talk of logical (tree-like) circulation diagrams, hierarchies of space in orderly sequence and the analysis of the so-called 'problems' contained in the brief for a building. The site at Minster Lovell Mill and the Client Committee, especially Tony Ambrose and Kit Ounstead, combined to defy these shibboleths. Kit Ounsted, who ran the Park Hospital in Oxford, had his own building team there to try out the effects of routes and spaces upon his particularly sensitive clients who were autistic children.

He told me that the ideal conference centre or meeting place would have more than one route to every place and a view out of each place in more than one direction so that you could choose who you wished or needed to encounter without giving offence, and so you could circulate comfortably. Tony Ambrose, who had grown up in the Mill, simply told me that the barn should contain meeting rooms; the house, dining room, common room, kitchen and offices; and the malthouse should contain the library; for no better reason than that was what they were best suited for, practically and sensually; not a surprising idea today but very much so in the analytical sixties.

The planners added to this by saying that people could come in at the village end of the site but that cars should come in at the other end, a quarter of a mile away: and the lovely Cotswold buildings and the mature garden beside the river Windrush made their own powerful presence felt.

So the new buildings at Minster Lovell are extensions of, and connections between, existing buildings in three ways. They take the three dimensional geometry of the existing buildings, being the way in which they occupy space, and develop and extend it to make the roofs over new buildings of modern timber, concrete and glass construction. They make new routes and paths, upstairs and down, that pass the doors to places in both old and new.

They complete and enhance and make connections through and across the waterside, landscaped garden.

Minster Lovell takes an old place and makes a new whole.

The unbuilt scheme in Oxford on page 78 also takes a highly prized historic place and builds with respect to its demands. A corner of the gardens of Worcester College, the lake and the playing fields all abut by a street corner that is just outside the College. Three towers of students' and fellows' rooms make beneath them gateways to the garden, to the playing fields, to the world outside. An L shaped grass topped terrace over further rooms has on it a belvedere overlooking the lake and makes two sides of a courtyard. The other two sides are built in embryo as a wall and a row of columns, awaiting further development of rooms or houses or apartments.

Page 79 illustrates the conversion of the old gym at Winchester College into a theatre workshop and the conversion of the old sanatorium into an Arts Centre. In both cases single new elements are added to transform the nature and the use of the building: at the theatre a porch which has the same section as the building, turns the axis and welcomes audiences: at the Arts Centre a new gallery between the two old sanatorium blocks makes connections, covers entrances and makes a new centre to which the sides are drawn.

Finally, the Uplands Conference Centre is shown on pages 80 to 85. A symmetrical house on a hilltop has been stripped of its many rambling and rather battered additions and is restored as a hall and four South-facing social rooms and meeting rooms on each of its two floors. It becomes the centrepiece and the pivot for a much larger composition. The hall is extended Northwards through a new two-storey grand hall that leads on North to dining rooms downstairs, seminar rooms up. Link blocks of bedrooms stretch East and West of the house and beyond the links are two pavilions. By foot, you can enter the building on axis; by car, you park under the trees and proceed direct or via the maze to any room or to the central hall where the reception desk is. The symmetry of the original house is respected, asymmetrical movement accepted.

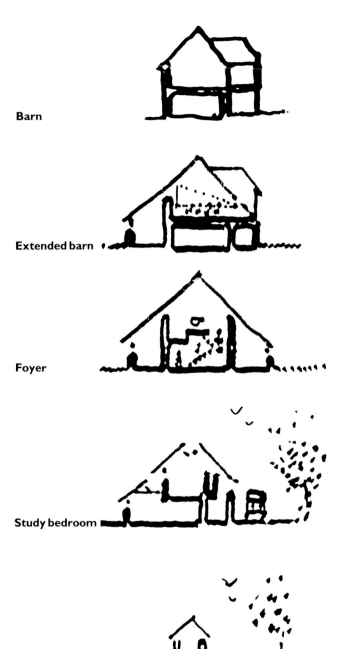

Barn

Extended barn

Foyer

Study bedroom

Cloister

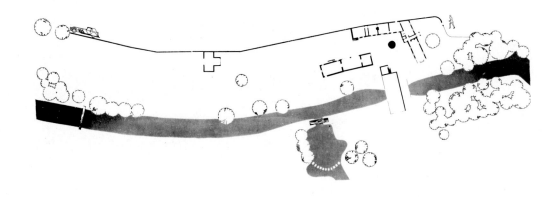

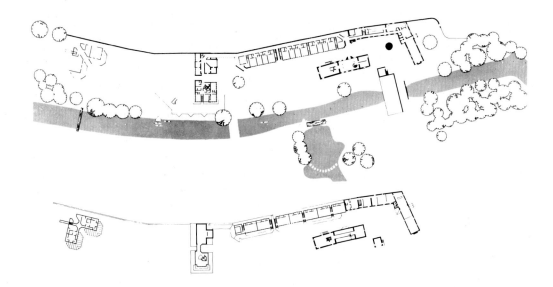

1968 **MINSTER LOVELL** **Edward Cullinan**
Julyan Wickham
Julian Bicknell

1980

WORCESTER COLLEGE

Edward Cullinan
Giles Oliver
Sunand Prasad

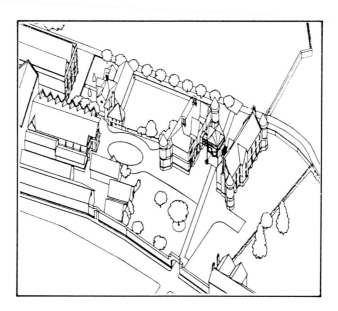

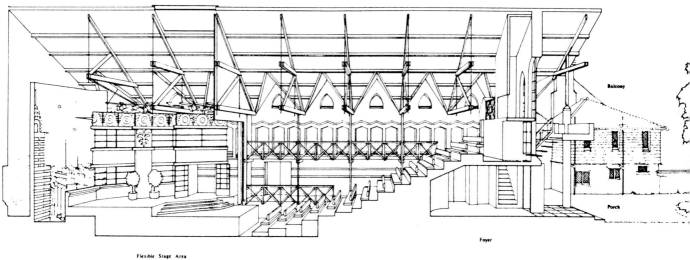

Balcony

Porch

Foyer

Flexible Stage Area

1982

WINCHESTER COLLEGE

Edward Cullinan
Anthony Peake
Alan Short

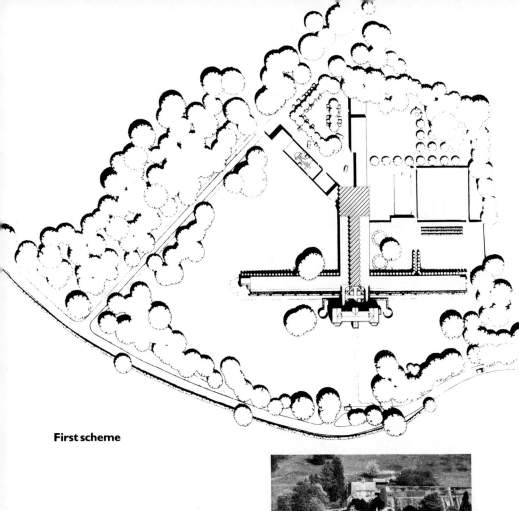

First scheme

1982-4

UPLANDS

Edward Cullinan
Anthony Peake
Mark Beedle
Alan Short
Sunand Prasad
Michael Chassay

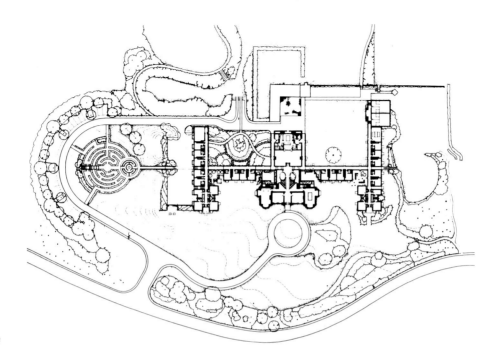

Built scheme

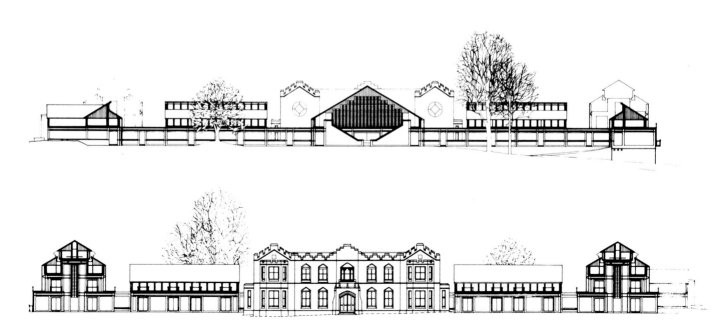

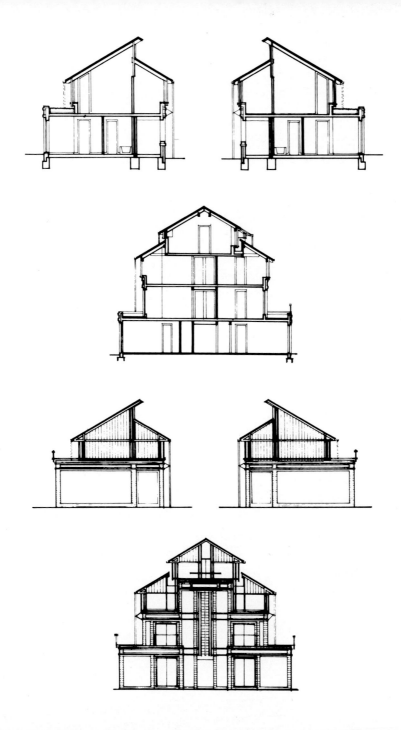

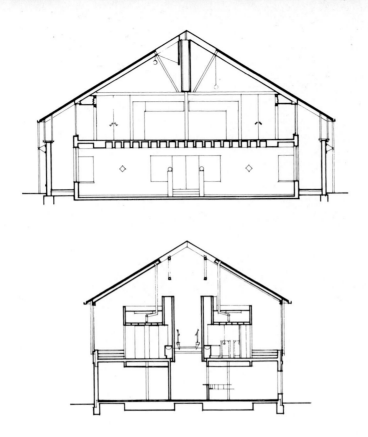

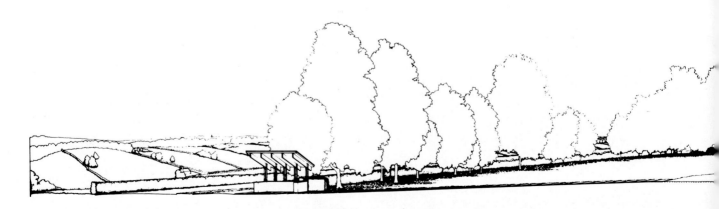

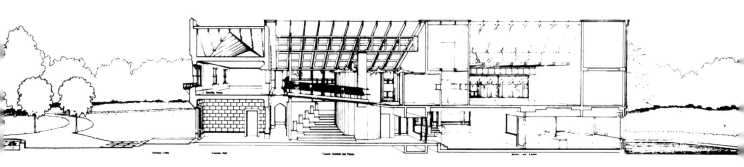

**Palladio's
Palazzo
Thiene**

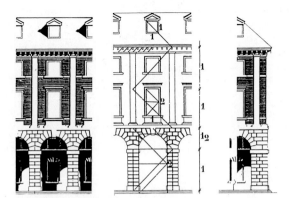

**Inigo Jones' original Covent Garden
Piazza elevations**

**Clutton's
Bedford
Chambers**

**Clutton's
Russell
Chambers**

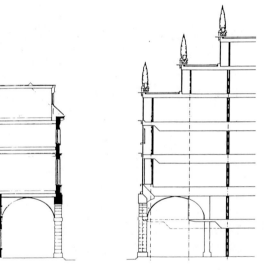

**Section through
Inigo Jones' Arcade**

**A possible section and elevation
for the new building**

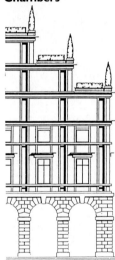

1984

A PROPOSAL FOR THE GARDEN

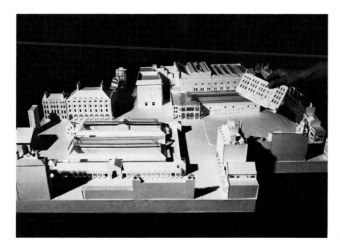
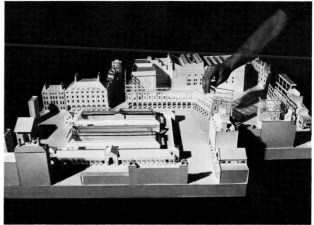
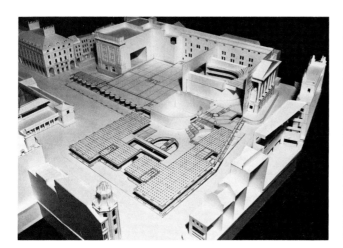

In 1983 the Board of the Royal Opera House Covent Garden invited architects to establish their ability to modernise the backstage parts of the Opera House and to develop new foyers, shops, restaurants, offices, and apartments to the side of it.

In 1984 four were asked to make proposals, this is ours:
A Garden Arcade combines an extension to the foyers with the public and commercial activities of Covent Garden market, the whole surmounted by a formal garden that hangs above 'The Garden' itself.

Our scheme was not chosen by the selectors.

6: Working with new ones

In Hampshire and Gloucestershire, there are about two hundred system-built (SCOLA) school buildings that were built between the fifties and the mid-seventies to accommodate what is crudely called 'the post-war baby bulge'. In other counties there are thousands more. They were built very fast and for small sums of money and although their authors were not very given to describing their work in aesthetic terms, I think it fair to say that they employed a quite definite aesthetic that could be called 'late Bauhaus reductivist'.

The earlier versions of the system were the purer and the more elegant versions, coming closer to the elegant and composed qualities of the Bauhaus originals; later ones tended towards tile hanging and other such 'soft' interventions.

The buildings were laid out on their sites as a series of blocks and linked blocks; as objects in space rather than as subjects that could form the edges of spaces, so they always had a lot of difficulty when it came to making the outdoors add up to more than the jelly between buildings. It is interesting that the object-like layouts themselves were seldom done with the dedication of, say, Mies' I.I.T. campus which does achieve a continuous quality of outdoor place thereby and in the opposite way.

Since the buildings were cheaply built from steel and glass and asbestos and painted wood, and the aesthetic smooth and reductivist and without overhangs, the problems that have arisen are fairly imaginable. They leak through the flat roofs, the softwood and the hardwood on the facades rots, they are under-insulated and they suffer from heat-loss through the glass on one side and too much solar gain on the other.

At Fleet school in Hampshire (pages 89 to 91), we have attempted to deal with these problems by respecting the orthogonal aesthetic of the original but by extending it and lightening it and making it both more delicate and more expressive.

The existing three-storey science building is re-insulated and re-roofed with a colour coated steel sandwich, over the top of and without disturbing the original. The new roof extends a metre and a half out from the face of the building to protect the walls and shade the windows, and this overhang is supported on poles which at ground level are supported on columns. At intermediate floors, these poles support shades above all windows for water shedding and sun control; opaque for sun control on the South side, translucent on the East and West sides, and transparent on the North.

Two new buildings, for drama, cinema and mathematics are placed at right angles to the science building, on either side of it. With walls of cypress trees and avenues of deciduous trees and by redirecting paths, two new outdoor courts are made that have a strong feeling of outdoor 'place'. At the end of one of the new buildings, at its intersection with the avenue of trees, is a covered bus-stop for the school. The new buildings use roofs and shades in the same way as in the science building, to protect its walls; but in the new buildings this protection is exploited to allow the highly insulated walls to be of strongly coloured, strongly patterned and layered plywood.

Fleet School is nearly finished and we are now looking at two more.

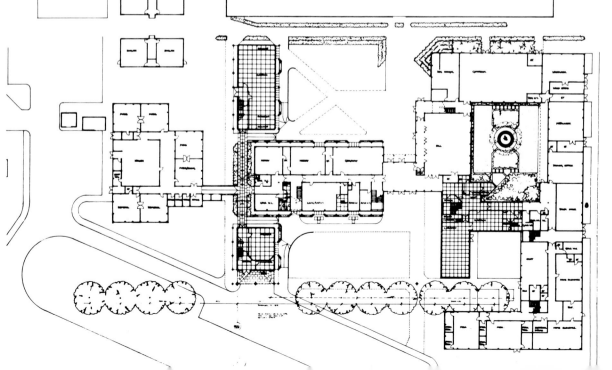

1983

FLEET SCHOOL

Edward Cullinan
Anthony Peake
Alan Short
Gregory Penoyre
Alexandra Freemantle

7: Then and now

On the left hand page is the plan of the upper floor of the Bell Tout lighthouse which I rebuilt in the fifties following its bombardment during the war. The floor of the new work is a rectangular platform dented by the old tower. The divisions on the floor are a response to the tower.

On the right-hand page is the plan of an old people's day care centre in Streatham, on which Robin Nicholson, Mungo Smith and I are now at work. The partly circular court, which is dented by the meeting rooms, is a hollow in the middle of the building, and main rooms and corridor open to it. The

caretaker's house is a solid circle that makes the street corner strong and pivots the entrance into the building and diagonally through to the court.

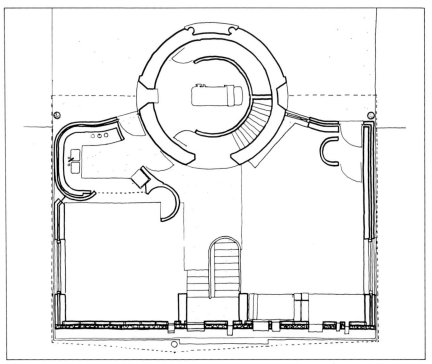

1955

LIGHTHOUSE   **Edward Cullinan**

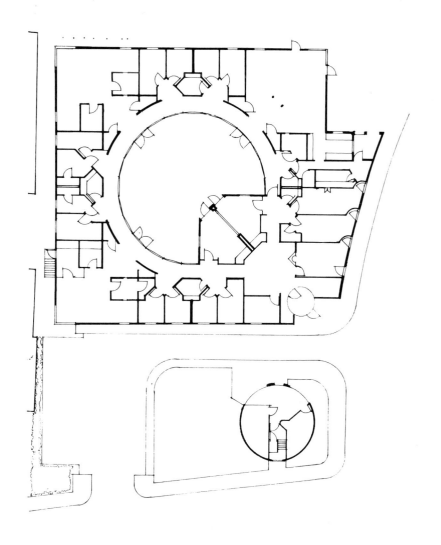

1984

DAY CARE CENTRE

Edward Cullinan
Robin Nicholson
Mungo Smith

Consultants and contractors

Chapter	Building	Quantity surveyor	Structural engineer	Services engineer	Main contractor
1: BUILDING THEM YOURSELF	**Hampshire**	—	—	—	Edward Cullinan and Horace Knight
	California	—	Patrick Moreau	—	Edward Cullinan
	London	—	Ove Arup	—	Edward Cullinan
2: MORE AND MORE HOUSES	**South Downs**	Stern & Woodford	S. Jampel & Partners	—	John C. Lillywhite
	Kawecki	—	—	—	Tom Pooley
	Garrett	—	S. Jampel & Partners	—	E. G. Kirk & Son
	Highgrove	L. B. Hillingdon	Peter Brett Associates	L. B. Hillingdon	Gee Walker & Slater Ltd
	Bradwell Common 2	Dearle & Henderson	S. Jampel & Partners	Zisman Bowyer	Llewellyn Construction Ltd
	Leighton Crescent	Stern & Woodford	Peter Brett Associates	L. B. Camden	Farrow Construction Ltd
	Westmoreland Road	Stern & Woodford	Peter Brett Associates	Edward Cullinan Architects	Rush & Tompkins Ltd
	Nelson Lodge	Dearle & Henderson	S. Jampel & Partners	Dearle & Henderson Max Fordham & Partners	A. J. Dunning & Sons (Weyhill) Ltd
3: WORKSHOPS	**Olivetti branches:**				
	– Belfast	Stern & Woodford	S. Jampel & Partners	Max Fordham & Partners	John Laing Construction Ltd.
	– Carlisle	Stern & Woodford	S. Jampel & Partners	Max Fordham & Partners	Miller Construction Ltd
	– Derby	Stern & Woodford	S. Jampel & Partners	Max Fordham & Partners	Ford & Weston Ltd
	– Dundee	Stern & Woodford	S. Jampel & Partners	Max Fordham & Partners	Bett Bros. Ltd
	Westoning Manor	M. K. Boyden & Co	S. Jampel & Partners	Fulcrum Consulting Engineers	T & B (St Albans) Ltd

Chapter	Building	Quantity surveyor	Structural engineer	Services engineer	Main contractor
4: DESIGNING WITH DISCUSSION	**Barnes Parish Church**	Stern & Woodford	S. Jampel & Partners	Max Fordham & Partners	W. S. Try Ltd
	Adventure Playground	Stern & Woodford and Edward Cullinan Architects	S. Jampel & Partners	Max Fordham & Partners	A. G. Case & Sons (London)
	Lambeth Hospital	Axtell Yates Hallett	F. J. Samuely & Partners	Max Fordham & Partners	Walter Lawrence & Son
5: WORKING WITH OLD BUILDINGS	**Minster Lovell**	Stern & Woodford	S. Jampel & Partners	Troughton & Young	Hinkins & Frewin
	Worcester College	Dearle & Henderson	—	—	—
	Winchester College	Stern & Woodford	F. J. Samuely & Partners	—	Mason & Co (Winchester) Ltd
	Uplands	Stern & Woodford	S. Jampel & Partners	Drake & Scull Ltd.	Benfield & Loxley Ltd
6: WORKING WITH NEW BUILDINGS	**Fleet School**	Willis & Thompson	S. Jampel & Partners	Max Fordham & Partners	H. N. Edwards & Partners
7: NOW AND THEN	**Bell Tout Lighthouse**	—	—	—	Llewellyn Construction Ltd
	Day Care Centre	Wilson Colbeck & Partners	Harris & Sutherland	—	Wates Special Works Ltd

BIBLIOGRAPHY

'A Studio near Petersfield'
House & Garden, May 1963

'Olivetti Hove'
Architectural Review, September 1971

'Olivetti Branch Offices, Edinburgh'
Architectural Review – Preview, January 1973

'Olivetti's New Branches in England'
Architectural Design, April 1973

'Quattro Filiali Olivetti in Inghiterra'
Domus, Milan, November 1973

'Olivetti's New Branches'
A + U, February 1974

'Two for Olivetti'
Architectural Review, April 1974

'Pick of the Projects – Highgrove'
Architectural Design, May 1974

'Industrial Building – Olivetti at Derby'
Architecture East Midlands, May 1974

'Study Centre, Minster Lovell, Oxfordshire'
Architectural Review, July 1976

'Olivetti Aujourdhui'
L'Architecture d'Aujourdhui, Paris, December 1976

'Building Study – Highgrove Housing'
Architects' Journal, July 1977

'British Architecture'
Architectural Design, September/October 1977

'Edward Cullinan Architects 1959-77'
Architectural Design, September/October 1977

'Unbuilt Britain'
A + U, Tokyo, October 1977

'Cullinan and Hillingdon'
RIBA Journal, February 1978

'Unique Synthesis of Past and Present' (Westmoreland Road)
Building Design, 5 October 1979

'MK Two Housing'
Building Magazine, March 1980

'Worcester College, Oxford'
Architects' Journal, May 1980

'A Decade of British Housing '70s'
The Toshi-Jutaku, Tokyo, October 1980

'London, Post Modern Architecture – A New House in Leighton Crescent'
Abitare, July/August 1981

'Edificio per Abitazioni nel Kent'
L'industria delle Construzioni No. 121, Milan, 1981

'St Mary Barnes' and 'A Question of Style'
Spazio e Società, Milan, January 1982

'Beautiful Barnes'
Architects' Journal, March 1982

'Two Projects by Edward Cullinan Architects'
(Workshop at Westoning and Charlie Chaplin Adventure Playground)
Architects' Journal, June 1982

'Gymnastic Conversions'
Theatre at Winchester College
Architects' Journal, March 1983

'St Barns Church' (sic)
Arkitektnytt. Oslo, 1983

'Adventure Playground in London' and 'Workshops for the Handicapped at Westoning'
Baumeister, Munich, August 1983

'The Cullinan Phenomenon – The Act and Art of Building'
Architectural Review, September 1983

'RIBA Variety Show – Hostel at Basingstoke'
Architects' Journal, October 1983

'Study-Centre in Minster Lovell, Oxfordshire'
Detail, Munich, November/December 1983

'Hostel at Basingstoke'
Architectural Review – Preview, January 1984

Bob Allies
'Saving Grace – Reformation of the Church at Barnes'
Architects' Journal, April 1984

Peter Cook and John Whale
'Barnes Continuity'
Architectural Review, May 1984

'Barnes Church Construction'
Building Magazine, June 1984

'Royal Opera House'
Architects' Journal, July 1984

'Down at Uplands'
Architects' Journal, August 1984

'The Cullinan Collection'
Article on exhibition at RIBA Heinz Gallery, London
Architects' Journal, 12 September 1984

Charles Knevitt
'The Designer as Master Builder. Show for Architect who won Royal praise'
The Times, 12 September 1984

Jan Burney
'Cullinan Concepts'
Building Design, 14 September 1984

Colin Amery
'Legacy of the swinging sixties'
The Financial Times, 24 September 1984

PRACTICE DETAILS

Since 1970 we have been organised by:

Mariette Smith
October 1970 to August 1972

Deborah Strother
September 1972 to January 1975

Claire Herniman
February 1975 to date

Since the practice was founded the following have also helped us:
Atalanta Beaumont
Tony Belcher
Anne Brandon-Jones
Angus Brown
Dominic Cullinan
Ros Cullinan
Keith Dabson
Lyn Danvers
David Dennis
Carl Falk
Susan Ford
Wendy Garrett
Séan Harrington
Michael Kozdon
Annette Main
Victoria Manser
Pete McGough
John Money-Kyrle
Angela Newman
Frans Nicolas
Bridie O'Dwyer
Dennis Pierperz
Amanda Potts
Julia Semler
Elizabeth Shapiro
Ron Smith
Hetty Startup
Peter St John
Jasper Vaughan
Charlie Wickham
Julia Wilson-Jones